BANGOR
TO
PORTMADOC

Vic Mitchell and Keith Smith

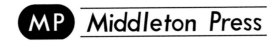
MP Middleton Press

Front cover: Ex-LMS 2-6-4T no. 42077 stands at the ticket platform just outside Llanberis station. Regular excursions were operated from Llandudno Junction and Rhyl. (Ted Hancock Railway Photographs)

Back cover upper: Caernarvon had a class 08 present in June 1969 to shunt the special trains run for the Investiture of the Prince of Wales. The coaches were for security staff, while the DMU was running normally. (K.Robinson)

Back cover lower: Caernarvon was reopened following the Britannia Bridge fire in May 1970, when freight for Holyhead and Ireland was transferred to road vehicles here. (K.Robinson)

Published April 2010
First reprint October 2015

ISBN 978 1 906008 72 7

© Middleton Press, 2010

Design Deborah Esher
Typesetting Barbara Mitchell

Published by
Middleton Press
Easebourne Lane
Midhurst
West Sussex
GU29 9AZ
Tel: 01730 813169
Fax: 01730 812601
Email: info@middletonpress.co.uk
www.middletonpress.co.uk

Printed in the United Kingdom by IJ Graphics, Guildford, Surrey. GU4 7WA

CONTENTS

INDEX

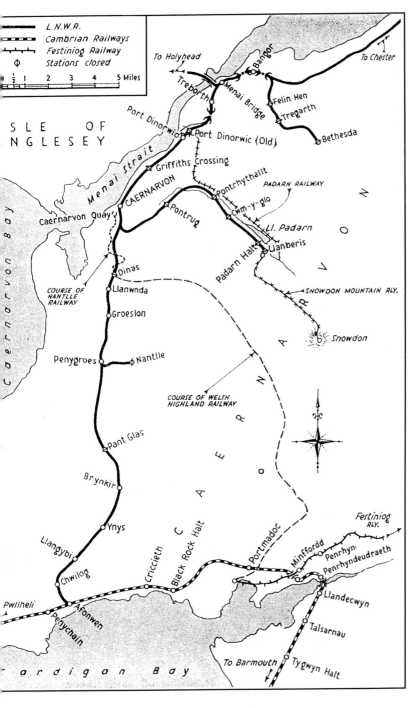

I.   The route diagram from 1958 shows the pre-1922 line ownership. (Railway Magazine)

ACKNOWLEDGEMENTS

We are very grateful for the assistance received from many of those mentioned in the credits also to B.Bennett, A.R.Carder, G.Croughton, M.Dart, F.Hornby, P.Jones, N.Langridge, B.Lewis, Mr D. and Dr S.Salter and in particular, our always supportive wives, Barbara Mitchell and Janet Smith. Much data has been obtained from the records and researches of W.G.Rear, but sadly he died as work began on this album.

GEOGRAPHICAL SETTING

The historic commercial centre of Bangor is set in a small but deep valley parallel to the northern end of the Menai Strait. The Chester to Holyhead line was built across this valley and thus the station is flanked by tunnels.

Our route to Caernarfon is roughly parallel to the Menai Strait and runs on the foothills of Snowdonia. The geology is ancient and complex; it includes both extrusive lavas and igneous rocks, such as granite and metamorphic rock, slate. The areas of workable slate are east of the route and were generally linked to it by narrow gauge railways.

The Llanberis branch followed the course of the Afon Rhythallt to this town, which is noted for its massive slate quarries at Dinorwic and the tourist attraction of the highest mountain in Wales, Snowdon.

Caernarfon is situated on a strategic headland at the west end of the Menai Strait and this promontory necessitated a short tunnel, as docks and quays occupied the waterfront. The route continues south and climbs over the east end of the Lleyn Peninsular, to reach Cardigan Bay. All the lines were situated in Caernarvonshire.

The maps are to the scale of 25ins to 1 mile, with north at the top, unless otherwise indicated. Welsh spelling and hyphenation has varied over the years and so we have generally used the form used by the railways at the time.

HISTORICAL BACKGROUND

The earliest line in the area was the Nantlle Railway, which ran from the slate quarries near Nantlle to a quay at Carnarvon. It opened in 1828 and was of 3ft 6ins gauge. Passengers were carried in about 1856-65.

The Chester & Holyhead Railway reached Bangor from Chester in 1848 and trains began running over the Menai Bridge in 1850. A junction was established east of it on 1st March 1852,

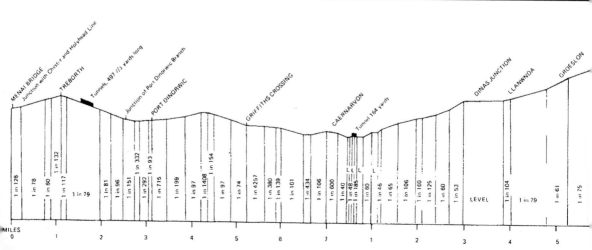

when mineral trains began to run to Port Dinorwic over the Bangor & Carnarvon Railway. This spelling was used in its Act of Parliament on 20th May 1851. Passenger services to Carnarvon began on 1st July 1852 and the line was soon leased to the C&HR. The routes became part of the London & North Western Railway in 1867.

The Carnarvonshire Railway's Act was dated 29th July 1862, but only the line south to Afon Wen was built. This opened on 2nd September 1867, the Cambrian Railways having completed the coastal section to Portmadoc, also in that year. The Carnarvonshire Railway acquired the Nantlle Railway under an Act of 29th July 1862 and relaid it to standard gauge on a straighter alignment. The part east of Talysarn remained horse-worked on the old track. The northern terminus was at Pant, south of Carnarvon, until 1st August 1870.

The Carnarvon & Llanberis Railway was authorised on 14th July 1864 and an extension under the former town came in another Act on 5th July 1865. The main route opened on 1st July 1869 and was worked by the LNWR. The part under the town came into use on 5th July 1870, the temporary station at Morfa closing on 1st August 1870. The LNWR absorbed the branch in that year and Carnarvon then had one station, instead of three.

Two narrow gauge lines came to the route from the east. The Padarn Railway joined it at Port Dinorwic, bringing slates from the Llanberis area. Its main route was of 4ft gauge from 1848, but a narrower horse-worked line was in use from 1824. The PR did not carry passengers, except workmen, and closed on 27th October 1961. The eastern part of it reopened (formally) on 28th May 1971 as the Llanberis Lake Railway, now a 2ft gauge pleasure line, 2½ miles in length. A full service began on 19th July 1971.

Operating from Dinas Junction from 21st May 1877 was the 2ft gauge North Wales Narrow Gauge Railway. It carried passengers from 15th August 1877, as far as Snowdon Ranger. Its complex history is told elsewhere, but to summarise, its name became the Welsh Highland Railway in 1922 and the route was extended to Portmadoc in 1923. It closed to passengers in 1936 and totally in 1937. A fresh WHR was created and a passenger service was provided in the tourist seasons from 1997 between Caernarfon and Dinas on the former LNWR route, using the name Rheilffordd Eryri. It was subsequently extended southwards on the old WHR route, in stages.

The LNWR became part of the London Midland & Scottish Railway in 1923, this becoming the London Midland Region of British Railways upon nationalisation in 1948.

The Llanberis branch closed to regular passenger traffic on 12th September 1932 and the Nantlle likewise on 8th August of that year. Such trains ceased between Caernarvon and Afon Wen on 7th December 1964 and between Bangor and Caernarvon on 5th January 1970. Freight withdrawals are detailed in the captions.

The routes were all single track, except Menai Bridge to Caernarfon. This was double from 1876 to 1966. The line south of Caernarfon station comprised two parallel single tracks for almost one mile.

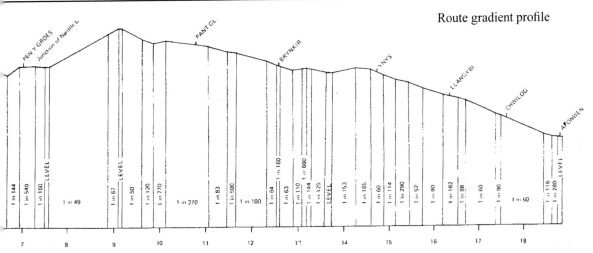

Route gradient profile

PASSENGER SERVICES

Nantlle Railway
The timetable was erratic in horsedrawn days, Bradshaw showing none in some months, one on Saturdays in others, and often the service terminated at Pen-y-Groes and not Carnarvon. A replacement bus service operated from 12th June 1865 until 2nd September 1867.

Nantlle Branch
Early timetables had three or four trains, weekdays only, often with an extra one on Caernarvon market day, which was Saturday. Usually only the first down and the last up train ran through.

In 1899, there were seven weekday trains, with one extra on Saturdays. The figures were nine and three by 1925.

Bangor to Afon Wen
Down train frequency is shown, with Sunday trains in brackets: 1869: 5 (1), 1899: 9 (1), 1928: 9 (0), 1950: 9 (0) and 1963: 8 (0). There were several extras as far as Caernarvon, particularly on Sundays in the 1930s.

There were through trains from Liverpool Lime Street and London Euston to Pwllheli and/or Portmadoc, one or two on Summer weekdays or just Saturdays. The Euston-Portmadoc coaches were part of "The Welshman" from 1950 to 1963, although they ran without a name in 1964. It was weekdays only: 11.15am depart and 6.15pm arrive.

Llanberis Branch
There were four or five trains, weekdays only, for most of the life of the line, with one or two extras on market days in some years. However, the service did improve in the 1920s, reaching nine return trips. There was an interesting final gasp in 1936-39, when a service was provided on Saturdays between Caernarvon and Padarn Halt only.

(Reproductions of three historical timetables are shown below.)

June 1869 — CARNARVONSHIRE timetable (S. Reay, Eus. Sts. London. / Traff. Man., Thos. Price.)

December 1873 — CARNARVONSHIRE. — London and North Western.

July 1918 — CARNARVON and LLANBERIS. — London and North Western.

* Station for Snowdon.

BANGOR, CAERNARVON, PENYGROES, and AFON WEN.

August 1928
July 1929
April 1932

Down, Week Days.

		mrn	aft	aft	aft	aft	aft	aft	aft	aft	aft
494 London (Euston)..dep.		5½50	9½20	12 35				2 35			
Bangor..........................dep.		4 48	8 53	10½43	11	11½10	1110	1130			
Menai Bridge		4 53	8 59	1046							
Treborth											
Port Dinorwic		5 4	9 10	1057							
Griffith's Crossing											
Caernarvon 501 ....arr.		5 14	9 17	11 6							
501 LLANBERIS ....arr.		8 10	10 1								
Caernarvon....................dep.		5 21	9 23	1110							
Dinas Junction 1079											
Llanwnda											
Groeslon											
Penygroes 540 ....{arr. dep.											
Pant Glas											
Brynkir											
Ynys											
Llangybi											
Chwilog B											
Afon Wen 141 ....arr.											
140 PWLLHELI ....arr.											
141 CRICCIETH ....arr.											
141 PORTMADOC ....arr.											
141 BARMOUTH ....arr.											

Sundays. One class only. — Thursdays and Saturdays. — Runs to Nantlle, see page 540. — Saturdays only. — Except Saturdays. One class only. — Through Carriages, Liverpool (Lime Street) to Afon Wen, see page 496. — Saturdays only. — Through Carriages to Pwllheli. — Through Express, London (Euston) to Pwllheli, Criccieth, and Portmadoc. — Through Carriages, Liverpool to Pwllheli, Criccieth and Portmadoc, see page 495. — Through Carriages, Manchester to Pwllheli, Criccieth, and Portmadoc, see page 495. — Saturdays only. One class only. — Through Carriages, Manchester to Pwllheli, Criccieth, and Portmadoc, see page 495. — Saturdays only. — Saturdays only. — Except Saturdays. Thro Train from Llandudno, see page 494.

Up, Week Days.

	mrn	aft	aft	aft	aft	aft	aft	aft	aft
140 BARMOUTH ....dep.									
140 PORTMADOC ....dep.									
141 CRICCIETH ....dep.									
141 PWLLHELI ....dep.									
Afon Wen ....dep.									
Chwilog B									
Llangybi									
Ynys									
Brynkir									
Pant Glas									
Penygroes 540 ....{arr. dep.									
Groeslon									
Llanwnda									
Dinas Junction 1079									
Caernarvon 501 ....{arr. dep.									
502 LLANBERIS ....dep.									
Caernarvon....................dep.									
Griffith's Crossing									
Port Dinorwic									
Treborth									
Menai Bridge									
Bangor B ....arr.									
499 London (Euston) ......arr.									

Saturdays only. Except Saturdays.

A Stops at 9 15 aft. on Sundays.
B Station for Four Crosses (2¾ miles), and Nevin (8¼ miles).
Bb Stops when required to take up for London.

A Stops at 9 15 aft. on Sundays.
B Station for Four Crosses (2¾ miles), and Nevin (8¼ miles).
Bb Mondays, Fridays, and Saturdays.

CAERNARVON and LLANBERIS (One class only), Week Days only.

Down.

Mls.		mrn	mrn	mrn	aft	aft	aft
—	Caernarvon .....dep.	7 45	9 26	11 6	1157		
3	Pont Rug						
5	Pontrhythallt	8 0	9 42	1117	1147		
6	Cwm-y-Glo						
9	Llanberis G 1079 ...arr.	8 10	9 52	1125	1155		

Up.

Through Train to Rhyl, see page 502b.				

Saturdays only. One class only. — Except Sats. Through Train to Rhyl, see page 502b. — Through Train to Llandudno, see p. 505b. — Through Express, Portmadoc, Criccieth, and Pwllheli to Liverpool, see page 501. — Through Express, Pwllheli to London. — Through Express, Portmadoc, Criccieth, and Pwllheli to Manchester, see page 502. — Thro' Exp. Pwllheli to Manchester, see p.500. — Through Express, Portmadoc, Criccieth, and Pwllheli to London (E.).

Cc Stops when required to take up from Manchester.
Dd Stops when required to take up for Birmingham and London.
E Except Saturdays.
F Stops to set down only.

Hh Stops when required to take up Saturdays only.
S Except Saturdays and 3rd instant.
V Saturdays; and on 3rd instant.

One class only.

BANGOR, CAERNARVON, PENYGROES, and AFON WEN.

Sundays.

	aft		
	1220		
	7 20		
	7 24		
	7 38		

Down, Week Days.

		mrn	aft	aft	aft	aft	aft	aft
494 London (E.) dep.		11 0						
Bangor ....dep.		10 30	4 10				1155	
Menai Bridge		4 17					1159	
Port Dinorwic								
Griffith's Crossing								
Caernarvon ....{arr. dep.							1214	
Dinas Junction 1079							1221	
Llanwnda								
Groeslon								
Penygroes 540 {arr. dep.								
Pant Glas								
Ynys								
Llangybi								
Chwilog B								
Afon Wen 141 ..arr.								

Sats. only. To Nantlle, see p. 540. — Except Thurs. and Sats. — Through Carriages, Liverpool (Lime Street) to Afon Wen, see page 496. — Through Carriages, London (Euston) to Pwllheli. — Through Carriages, Liverpool and Manchester to Pwllheli, Criccieth, and Portmadoc, see page 495.

Up, Week Days.

		mrn	aft	aft	aft	aft	aft
140 BARMOUTH ...dep.							
140 PORTMADOC ..dep.							
141 CRICCIETH ...dep.							
141 PWLLHELI ....dep.							
Afon Wen ....dep.							
Chwilog B							
Llangybi							
Ynys							
Brynkir							
Pant Glas							
Penygroes 540 {arr. dep.							
Groeslon							
Llanwnda							
Dinas Junction 1079							
Caernarvon ....{arr. dep.							
Griffith's Crossing							
Port Dinorwic							
Treborth							
Menai Bridge							
Bangor C 494, 499 .arr.							
499 London (E.) ...arr.							

Runs 15 mins. earlier on Saturdays. — Through Carriages, Pwllheli to London (Euston), see p. 500. — Through Carriages, Afon Wen to Liverpool (Lime Street), see p. 500.

Aa Stops to set down on informing Guard at preceding stopping Station, and to take up on giving notice at the Station.
B Station for Four Crosses (2¾ miles) and Nevin (8¼ miles). X Arr. 9 50 aft. on Sats.
C Station for Beaumaris (5 miles).
E Except Sats.   S Sats. only.

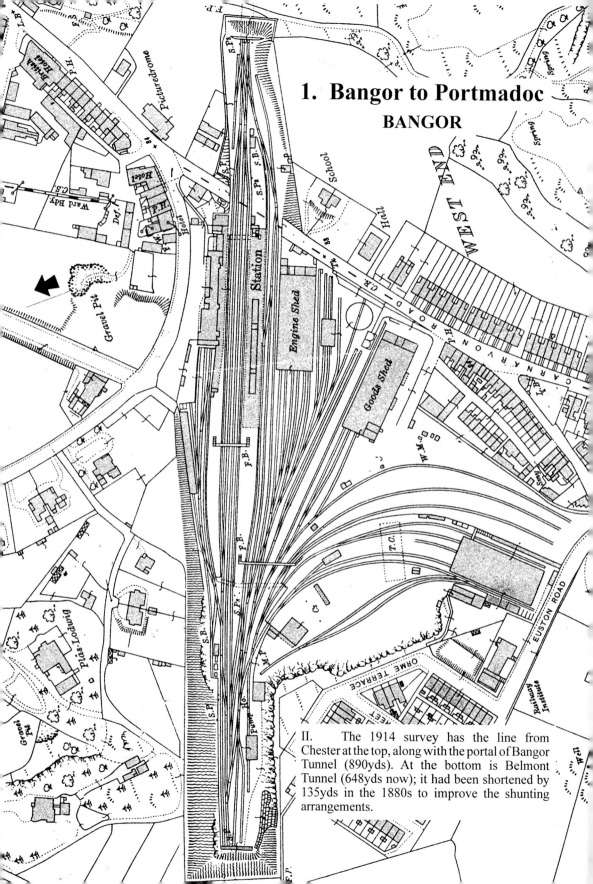

1. Bangor to Portmadoc
BANGOR

II. The 1914 survey has the line from Chester at the top, along with the portal of Bangor Tunnel (890yds). At the bottom is Belmont Tunnel (648yds now); it had been shortened by 135yds in the 1880s to improve the shunting arrangements.

Station

Engine Shed

Goods Shed

WEST END

CARNARVON ROAD

EUSTON ROAD

ORME TERRACE

Railway Institute

Plas Lodwig

Gravel Pit

Picturedrome

British Hotel

1.   This is the north elevation of the original building and its outline is on the map. It was isolated on the up platform after two tracks were laid in the foreground in the 1920s, creating an island platform. The British Hotel is top left on the map; it was only a short walk away. (Lens of Sutton coll.)

2.   The mouth of Bangor Tunnel is seen from the bridge over Carnarvon Road in 1939, along with No. 1 Box. This had 82 levers and was in use until 8th December 1968. (M.J.Stretton coll.)

3.	The locomotive depot is on the left of this westward view from the 1950s and No. 1 Box is in the foreground. The rebuilding in 1924-27 resulted in the provision of the two through lines on the right and a new entrance building north of them. It is linked to the platforms by a covered footbridge. The short bay platform on the left was used by Bethesda branch trains. (D.Lawrence/H.Davies coll.)

➔ 4.	The engine shed was LNWR no. 21 and became LMS no. 7B in 1935, being renumbered 6H by BR in 1952. It is seen in June 1956 and was closed on 12th June 1965, when there were only 15 engines remaining here. In the foreground is no. 52230, a class 3F 0-6-0 of a type introduced in 1889. There was a staff of 52 in 1952 and they had 29 engines, issued over 80,000 tickets, received 70,000 parcels and forwarded 25,000. There were 40 more men dealing with goods traffic. (H.C.Casserley)

5.   The 11.14 Llandudno Junction to Holyhead is arriving on 10th April 1999, by which time renovation of the original building, including a fenestrated chimney, had been undertaken. (P.G.Barnes)

6.	Seen on the same day is the 11.16 Bangor to Birmingham New Street, hauled by EWS no. 37401. There were few loco-hauled trains by that time. (P.G.Barnes)

↓ 7.	A panorama from 5th May 2009 reveals that the former No. 2 Box was still in use. Its 90 levers had been replaced by a panel. There was still a fan of sidings beyond the fence, but these were only used by Network Rail. The up platform (right) could take 11 coaches and the down one 13. Some publications carried the suffix (Gwynedd) from 1984. (V.Mitchell)

MENAI BRIDGE

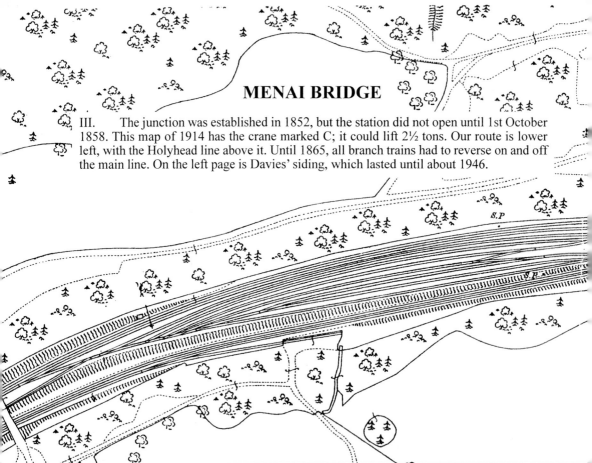

III.   The junction was established in 1852, but the station did not open until 1st October 1858. This map of 1914 has the crane marked C; it could lift 2½ tons. Our route is lower left, with the Holyhead line above it. Until 1865, all branch trains had to reverse on and off the main line. On the left page is Davies' siding, which lasted until about 1946.

8.   We look towards Bangor on an unknown date and see the 1865 platform on the right. The chimneys of the main building are on the left. An earlier station on the main line, further west, had been called Britannia Bridge. (J.Langford coll.)

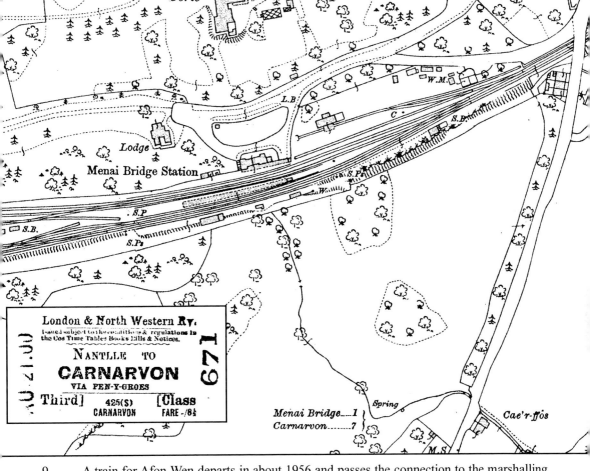

London & North Western Ry.

Issued subject to the conditions & regulations in the Cos Time Tables Books Bills & Notices.

NANTLLE TO

CARNARVON

VIA PEN-Y-GROES

Third] 425(S) [Class
CARNARVON FARE -/8½

671

9.   A train for Afon Wen departs in about 1956 and passes the connection to the marshalling yard. The map shows two signal boxes; the one in this vicinity lasted until about 1935. (J.W.T.House/C.L.Caddy coll.)

10. Ex-LMS 2-6-4T no. 42478 shunts freight from the branch in 1957, while more goods wait on the up main line. Beyond the sign 163 are steps to the subway. (J.W.T.House/C.L.Caddy coll.)

11. The main lines are featured in this view west and the signal box is behind us. It had 40 levers and closed on 9th December 1973. Passenger service ceased here on 14th February 1966 and the subway was filled in. (Lens of Sutton coll.)

12.   The up building was recorded on 19th July 1963, but it was destroyed after closure. Beyond the hut on the right is part of the goods shed. The yard closed on 28th January 1972 and an industrial estate was developed on its site. (R.M.Casserley)

For other views of Bangor station, please see
Rhyl to Bangor and *Bangor to Holyhead*.
This station also appears in the latter.

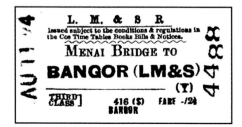

TREBORTH

IV.   The station was a little under one mile from the one just visited and the main line was close by, top left. The siding is gated, suggesting that it was private at the time of the survey in 1914. It was laid down in 1902. Passengers were conveyed from 1854 until 1st October 1858, but it was reopened within eight weeks, due to the rights of the local landowner.

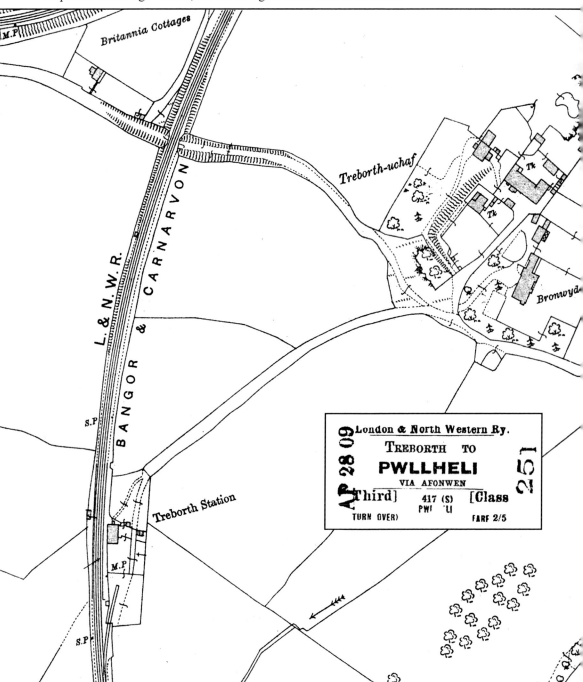

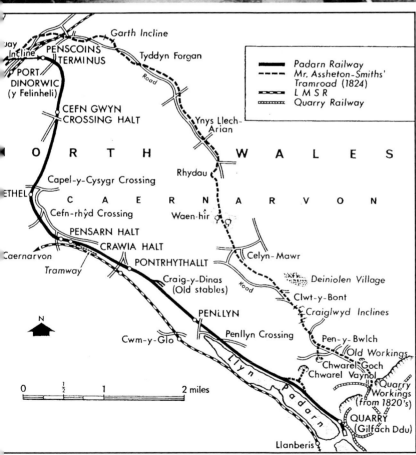

13. We look south in 1957, but the siding is obscured by the main building. Both passenger and freight services were withdrawn on 2nd March 1959, but the ground frame remained usable until 24th April 1966. (Stations UK)

V. The stations shown on the Padarn Railway were for the use of workmen only and its main line was of 4ft gauge. The tracks at each end were of a nominal 2ft gauge and the small wagons were carried on transporter wagons, in groups of four. The 60-seat coaches were attached and detached at each station, but were not used after November 1947.

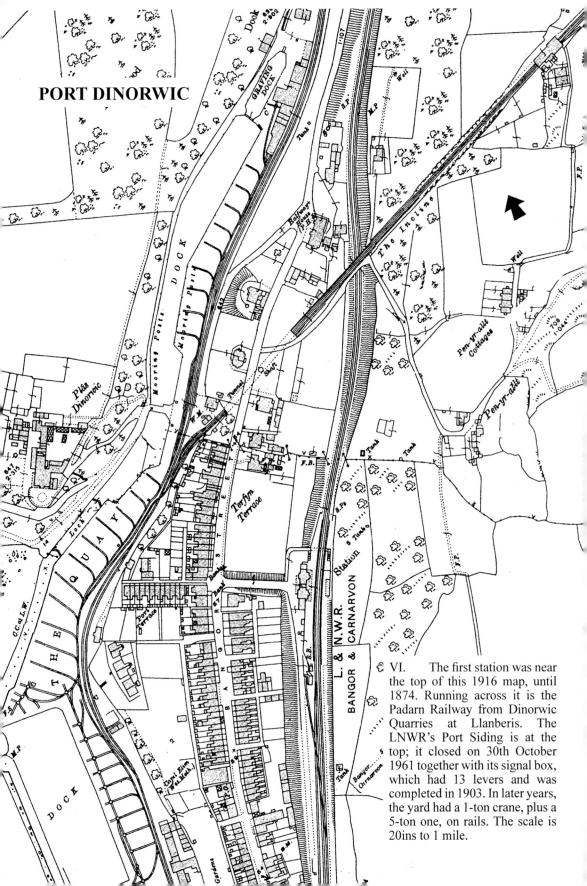

PORT DINORWIC

VI.   The first station was near the top of this 1916 map, until 1874. Running across it is the Padarn Railway from Dinorwic Quarries at Llanberis. The LNWR's Port Siding is at the top; it closed on 30th October 1961 together with its signal box, which had 13 levers and was completed in 1903. In later years, the yard had a 1-ton crane, plus a 5-ton one, on rails. The scale is 20ins to 1 mile.

14.   The grand styling appears to compete with the stations at Bangor and Menai Bridge. The nearest wing might take first prize in a competition for toilets for gentlemen and seems to confirm the need for prayer when enthroned. The signs each side announce the presence of a subway. Its third entrance is shown on the map. (Lens of Sutton coll.)

15.   At Port Dinorwic Quay, the Padarn Railway kept a narrow gauge (1ft 10¾ ins) locomotive for shunting and movements to and from the foot of the incline. On 28th August 1954 it was an Andrew Barclay 0-4-0WT of 1931, built as no. 1995. Behind it is 0-6-0 no. 52230. (H.C.Casserley)

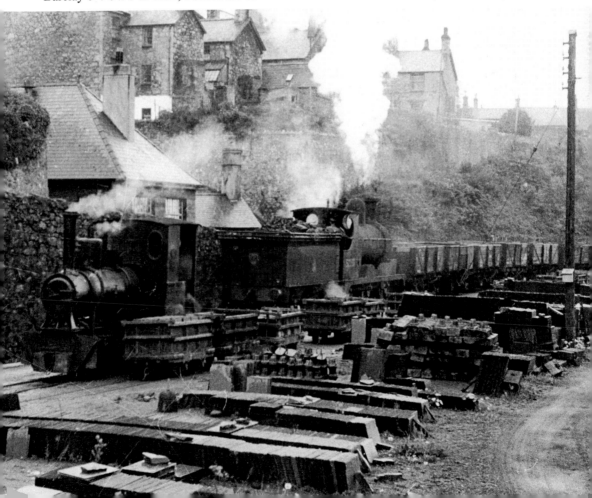

16.   A southward view on 24th August 1954 shows the access to the goods yard, which was open until 4th May 1964. The signal box had a frame with 18 levers and was built in 1903. (R.M.Casserley)

17.   The impressive northwest elevation was recorded on the same day. Sombre yellow bricks had been used. (R.M.Casserley)

18.   The station closed on 12th September 1960, but goods traffic continued until 4th May 1964. This photograph was taken between those dates. The signal box lasted until 24th June 1965. (Lens of Sutton coll.)

GRIFFITHS CROSSING

19.   Fame came on 13th November 1911 when temporary extensions were made for extra traffic for the Investiture of the then Prince of Wales. The locomotives are Experiment class LNWR 4-6-2Ts. Royalty travelled by road from here to be visible to the crowds. A wooden platform and footbridge were erected at Carnarvon for 26 extra trains. (LNWR)

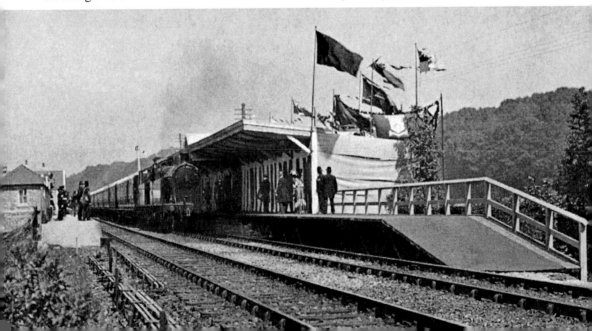

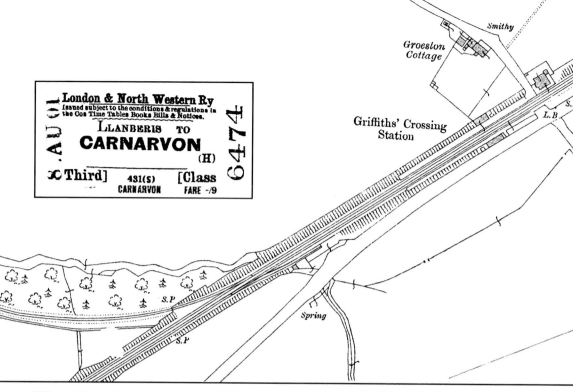

VII. The station opened in June 1854 and is seen on the 1917 edition. The curved siding ran to Parkia Brickworks. The site was later a petrol depot and subsequently had a concrete works on it. Some sleepers were produced therein.

20. The station closed on 5th July 1937 and this photograph was probably taken at that time. The goods yard was in use from 1874 until 6th July 1964. A cattle pen was provided.
(Railway Magazine)

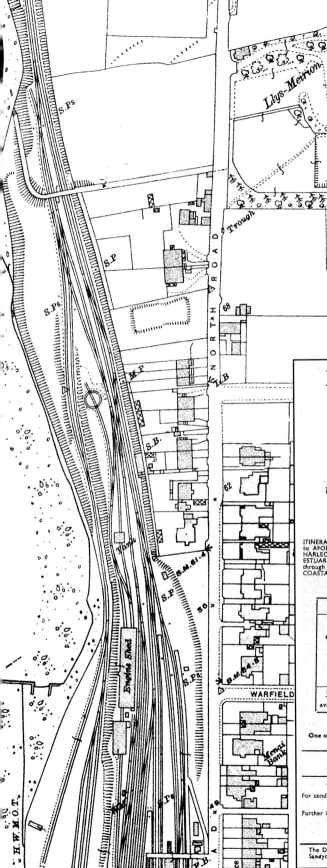

CAERNARVON

VIII. We begin our survey with three 1920 maps, in journey order. This includes the engine shed, which the LNWR numbered 21C. It housed eleven locomotives in 1921 and closed on 14th September 1931. No. 1 Box is marked S.B. and its 68-lever frame was in use until 24th April 1966.

To *SEE* North Wales Travel by Train

NORTH WALES LAND CRUISE

A Circular Rail Tour of the most magnificent scenery in North Wales

TUESDAYS   WEDNESDAYS & THURSDAYS
29th JUNE TO 2nd SEPTEMBER 1954

ITINERARY—CONWAY to BANGOR along the coast, thence via MENAI BRIDGE & CAERNARVON to AFONWEN and southwards following the CAMBRIAN COAST through PORTMADOC and HARLECH to BARMOUTH, where time is allowed for sightseeing. Return by the MAWDDACH ESTUARY, DOLGELLEY, BALA LAKE and through the VALE OF EDEYRNION to CORWEN, thence through the VALE OF CLWYD via RUTHIN and DENBIGH to RHYL from where the NORTHERN COASTAL ROUTE is followed to starting points.

OVER 150 MILES OF RESTFUL TRAVEL

Fare		From		Timetable
S D				**a m**
13/-		CONWAY	depart	9 35
		PENMAENMAWR	"	9 40
		LLANFAIRFECHAN	"	9 50
		BANGOR	"	10 05
		CAERNARVON	"	10 20
				p m
		BARMOUTH	arrive	12 20
		BARMOUTH	depart	2 15
		CONWAY	arrive	5 36
		PENMAENMAWR	"	5 44
Holiday Runabout Tickets are not available by this train		LLANFAIRFECHAN	"	5 51
		BANGOR	"	6 05
		CAERNARVON	"	6 25

BOOK IN ADVANCE—SEATS ARE LIMITED

One of the many thousands of delighted passengers states : "I cannot think of a more enjoyable way of seeing such marvellous scenery."

POPULAR PANTRY CAR SERVICE
Light Refreshments, Minerals, Ices, etc., obtainable on the train at nominal prices.

Children under three years of age free ; three years and under fourteen half-fares.

For conditions of issue of these tickets, also luggage allowances, see the Railway Bye-Laws and Regulations, Notices and Conditions of Issue of Tickets, etc.

Further information will be supplied on application to the Stations, Agencies, or to F. H. FISHER, District Traffic Superintendent, Chester Telephone Chester 24680 (Ext. 28).

The Deeside Printing Co., Sandycroft, Nr. Chester.

May. '54 BR 35001 K513

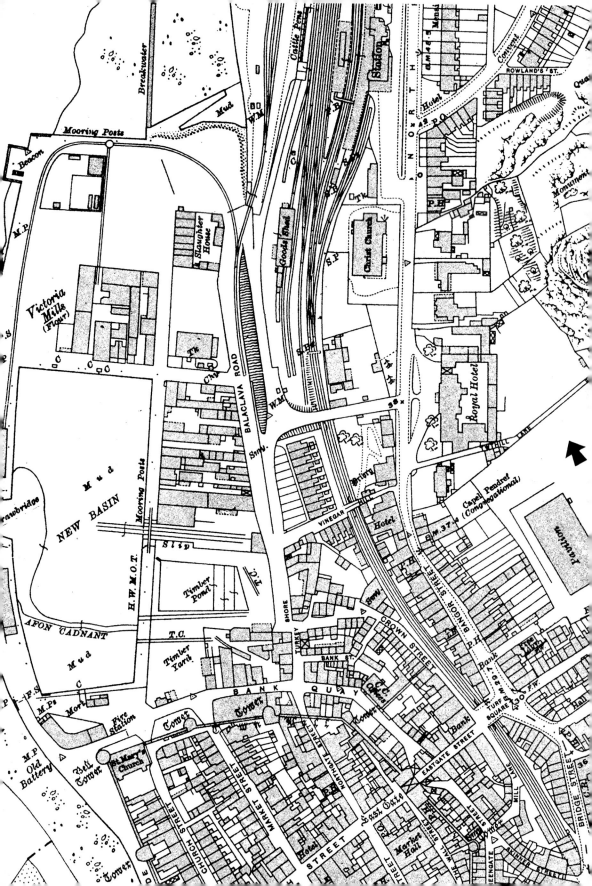

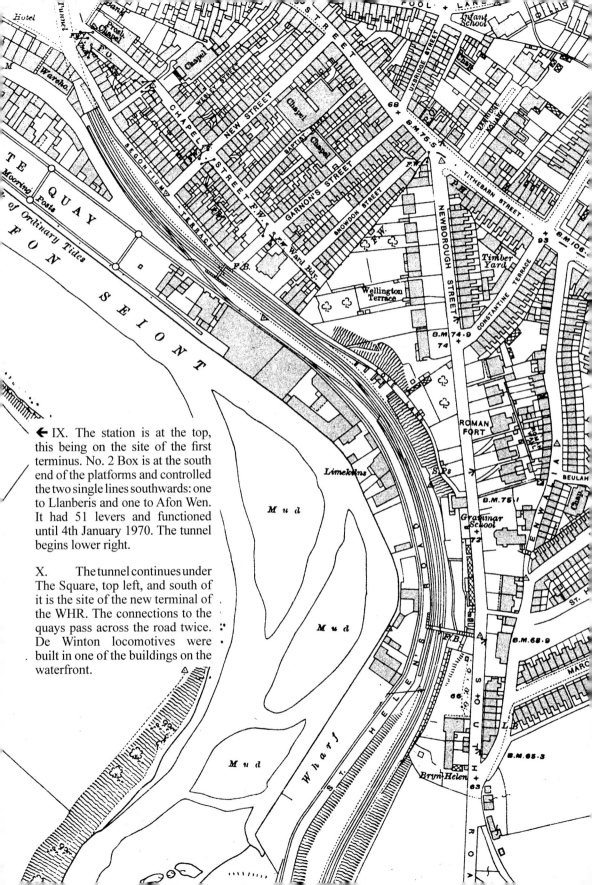

← IX. The station is at the top, this being on the site of the first terminus. No. 2 Box is at the south end of the platforms and controlled the two single lines southwards: one to Llanberis and one to Afon Wen. It had 51 levers and functioned until 4th January 1970. The tunnel begins lower right.

X.   The tunnel continues under The Square, top left, and south of it is the site of the new terminal of the WHR. The connections to the quays pass across the road twice. De Winton locomotives were built in one of the buildings on the waterfront.

21.   A postcard view from North Road from around 1900 features railway road transport of the era and the then still covered footbridge. The railway had six lorries here in the early 1950s. (Lens of Sutton coll.)

22.   An indifferent southward view in the 1930s emphasises the spelling used from 1925. The train in the centre is probably bound for Afon Wen. (Stations UK)

23.	A Sunday school excursion to Rhyl was recorded on 6th July 1950, hauled by nos 44742 and 40143. Tender engines were not commonly used on the route and former GWR ones usually only appeared on Land Cruise trains. (J.H.Meredith)

24.	Ex-LMS 2-6-4T no. 42418 waits to depart south in about 1957. There was a bay platform on the right, once used by Llanberis trains. (J.W.T.House/C.L.Caddy coll.)

26. Cattle wagons abound in this northward panorama from about 1960. Mailbags and gas lights add to the period atmosphere. The population of the town was steady at around 9000 folk. The wagons often came from Holyhead for cleaning out. Much of the weather protection was removed in 1956, when the building in the centre arrived. (Lens of Sutton coll.)

25.   Platform 6 had been a wooden excursion platform built in 1911, but it was little used after 1914, except by carriage cleaners. No. 3 was the most frequently used platform in the final years. No. 1 Box is in the distance in this northward view of terminal decline. The shabby premises were used for the special trains for the Investiture on 1st July 1969, although some of the eleven used a temporary platform, near the Ferodo Works. (Lens of Sutton coll.)

↓ 27. Public goods traffic was withdrawn on 4th August 1969 and passenger services followed on 5th January 1970. However, following fire damage to Britannia Bridge, the yard was reopened for the Irish container traffic from 15th June 1970 until 31st January 1972; see back cover. Compare this 1960s view with picture 21. The site was cleared for a Safeway supermarket. (T.David/C.L.Caddy coll.)

SOUTH OF CAERNARVON

28.   The south end of the tunnel is seen in the 1930s. It is now used by road traffic and a roundabout has been built in the foreground. It carries bidirectional traffic, but is fitted with emergency traffic lights. (R.S.Carpenter coll.)

→ 29.   Moving south in November 1964, we have the Llanberis line on the right and the Afon Wen route on the left. The castle and footbridge appear again in the next picture. (N.Kneale/M.J.Stretton coll.)

→   30. The terminus of the revived WHR is seen on 15th May 1999 as Garratt 2-6-6-2 no. NG143 backs onto a train, destined for Dinas. (V.Mitchell)

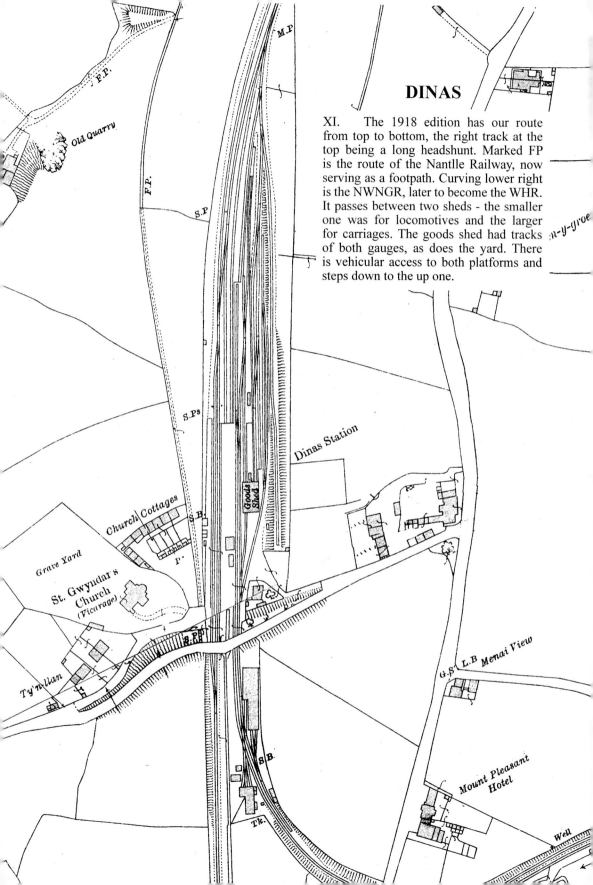

DINAS

XI. The 1918 edition has our route from top to bottom, the right track at the top being a long headshunt. Marked FP is the route of the Nantlle Railway, now serving as a footpath. Curving lower right is the NWNGR, later to become the WHR. It passes between two sheds - the smaller one was for locomotives and the larger for carriages. The goods shed had tracks of both gauges, as does the yard. There is vehicular access to both platforms and steps down to the up one.

Old Quarry

F.P.

F.P.

M.P.

S.P.

S.P.

S.Ps

Dinas Station

n-y-groe

Church Cottages

S.B.

Goods Shed

P.

Grave Yard

St. Gwyndai's Church (Vicarage)

Ty'n llan

S.P.

G.S L.B Menai View

S.B.

Mount Pleasant Hotel

Tk.

Well

31.   The station opened on 15th August 1877, along with the NWNGR, the track of which can be seen on the right of this 1909 photograph. That line closed in 1916 and reopened in 1922 as the WHR. The signal on the right did not survive the closure period. (R.M.Casserley coll.)

32.   The suffix "junction" was applied from 1912 until 26th September 1938. "Caerns" was added later. The buffet was operated by the Snowdon Mountain Railway at one period and it occupied the building on the left. This was used as an oil store after the WHR closure and later by the Methodist Church. (G.E.Hughes/WHR Heritage Group)

33. The WHR trackbed is in the foreground in this panorama from 26th April 1959. It includes an A35 van conversion. (A.M.Davies)

34. The WHR closed to passengers in September 1936 and for goods in July 1937. There was subsequently little traffic at this station. BR withdrew goods service on 10th September 1951. (Lens of Sutton coll.)

Other illustrations of this station are in *Branch Lines around Portmadoc 1923-46*, **which includes a journey on the WHR to that town.**

35. Passenger service was also withdrawn on 10th September 1951, but the loop and signal box remained in use until line closure. The loop had been extended in 1893 and again in 1947. This northward view is from about 1960, when one oil lamp remained to illuminate the signalman when passing trains.
(Lens of Sutton coll.)

36. The main building was immaculately restored by WHR volunteers and new coaches were built. Running round a departure for Caernarfon on 30th August 1998 is ex-South African Railways Garratt no. 143, which was built in Manchester in 1958. Service was extended to Waunfawr in 2000 and the station became a passing place again. (V.Mitchell)

LLANWNDA

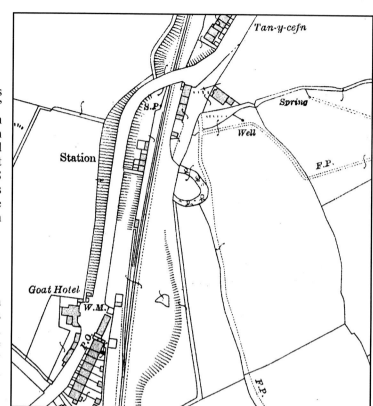

XII. The station was called "Pwllheli Road" until Dinas opened in 1877. The extent to which the road was diverted when the station was built is evident on this 1918 extract. W.M. indicates Weighing Machine. The population was 2107 in 1901.

37. A view south on 12th August 1953 has the ladies waiting room nearest. It appears to be an afterthought; many stations had provision only for gentlemen. (H.C.Casserley)

38.   The siding could accommodate five wagons, but there was seldom more than one. This would be loaded with ten tons of coal for the local merchant. The shed was for parcel traffic by passenger train. (R.S.Carpenter coll.)

39.   Another view from around 1960 and this includes the distant signal for Dinas. The goods yard closed on 4th May 1964, only months before line closure. The bridge was later demolished and the road restored to its original alignment. (R.S.Carpenter coll.)

GROESLON

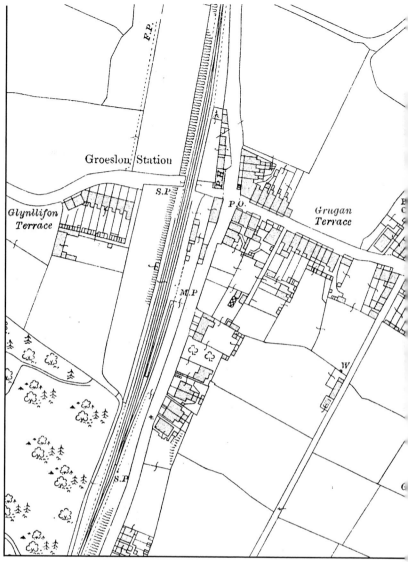

XIII. The 1918 edition has the main road running parallel to the railway. Buses would soon stop at the crossroads.

40. The parcels shed is nearest in this postcard view. The left platform and the loop were added in 1911 to increase line capacity.
(Lens of Sutton coll.)

Groeslon Station

Glynllifon Terrace

Grugan Terrace

41.   This is a southward view and departing trains would soon pass Tudor Siding, where slate was loaded. This was a private siding on the east side and it lasted until the end. (Lens of Sutton coll.)

42.   The loops on the route were lengthened in 1947 to accommodate ten-coach trains destined for Butlins, west of Afon Wen. Here it had to be carried beyond the level crossing, where the gates were hand operated. (R.S.Carpenter coll.)

43.   Features from a bygone era include the low-level paraffin lamp, a loading gauge and a set of portable steps to aid the less agile. (J.Moss/R.S.Carpenter coll.)

44.   The token machine was situated in the station building, but every other signalling component was in the open. The LNWR displayed this economy measure elsewhere - see our *Bletchley to Cambridge* album. The frame was in use until 4th May 1964. (J.Moss/R.S.Carpenter coll.)

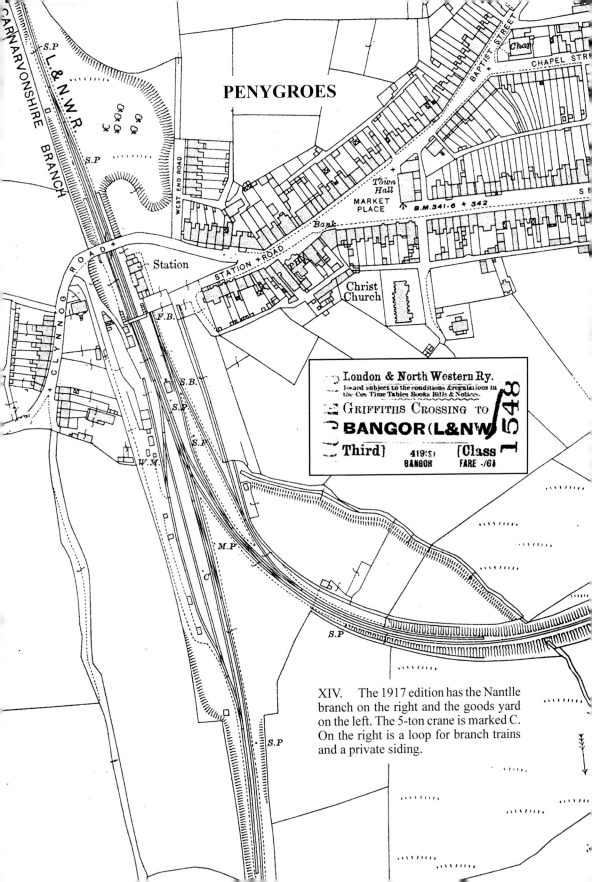

PENYGROES

CARNARVONSHIRE BRANCH

L. & N.W.R.

S.P

S.P

WEST END ROAD

CLYNNOG ROAD

Station

STATION ROAD

F.B.

S.B.

S.P

S.P

W.M.

M.P

C

S.P

S.P

Town Hall

MARKET PLACE

B.M. 341·6 + 342

Bank

P.H.

Christ Church

BAPTIST STREET

CHAPEL STR

Chap

London & North Western Ry.

Issued subject to the conditions &regulations in the Cos Time Tables Books Bills & Notices.

GRIFFITHS CROSSING TO

BANGOR (L&NW

Third]   419(S)   [Class
          BANGOR   FARE -/6¼

1548

XIV.   The 1917 edition has the Nantlle branch on the right and the goods yard on the left. The 5-ton crane is marked C. On the right is a loop for branch trains and a private siding.

45.   This poor quality postcard is included as it features a Nantlle train in the bay platform. Hyphens were used in the name until 1904. (Lens of Sutton coll.)

46.   The gardens often won prizes in district competitions. This is the first of four photographs from the late 1950s and this one has the branch points just beyond the signal box. (Lens of Sutton coll.)

47.   An up freight train is largely obscured by a train bound for Afon Wen behind 2-6-4T no. 42585. The lighting is by Suggs Rochester pattern gas lamps, which were shadow free. (Ted Hancock Railway Photographs)

48.   On the right is the former bay track and centre is the down line, which was signalled for reversible running, but seldom used by up trains. The signal box had 33 levers. (H.C.Casserley)

49.   The goods yard is on the right and it was in use until 4th May 1964, but it continued to be used by the local coal merchant thereafter. (J.Moss/R.S.Carpenter coll.)

50.   Nearest is the house for the station master and between it and the footbridge is his back yard, a concept lost in modern housing. At least his wife could dry their clothes in private. The photograph is from 17th July 1963. (R.M.Casserley)

51. At the opposite end of the building were the facilities for gentlemen and, unlike most railways, the LNWR provided full roofing. (R.M.Casserley)

52. The demolition train was recorded in 1968, behind no. D5020. A private road was laid on the trackbed here for lorries carrying stone and a cycleway followed. The A487 now runs along this part of the former route. (K.Robinson coll.)

NANTLLE

XV.   The 1916 edition has the line from Penygroes on the left. The 3ft 6ins gauge line is partially in tunnel top right at the start of the 1½ mile route to the slate quarries. Over 40 were recorded in the Nantlle district, but the station was in Talysarn. The Coed-Madog Quarry was in production in 1883-1908 and had three vertical-boilered 0-4-0s made by De Winton in Caernarvon. The LNWR siding above it was the only one in this valley to serve a quarry directly. Cloddfa'r Coed Quarry used it for small quantities. The parallel lines across the bottom of the map represent the straightened Afon Llynfi.

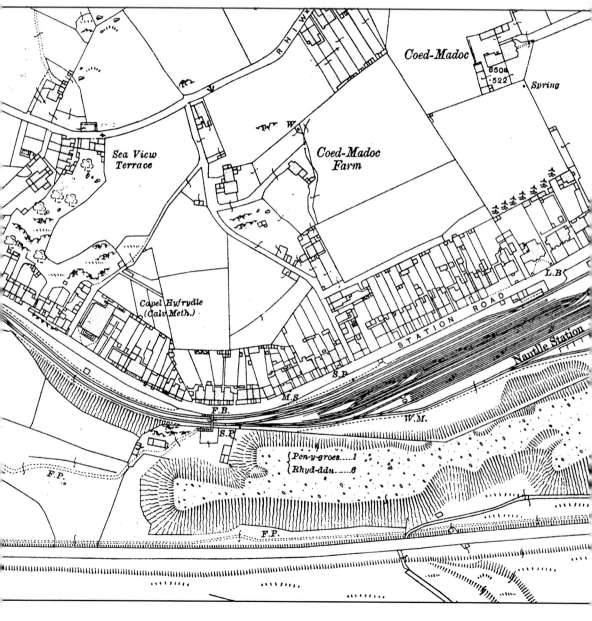

53.   Two photographs from a wet day in November 1952 set the scene. First we look east at the main building, which had not received a passenger for 20 years. (H.Ballantyne)

54.   We look west along the transfer sidings and 500yds beyond the footbridge were more; these were known as Tanrallt sidings. The points in the centre had pivotted rails, instead of blades. There had been a signal box in the distance until about 1900. (H.Ballantyne)

55.   There were four parallel narrow gauge lines in this group, with another two further south. This gave three transhipment platforms for slate transfer. No. 42366 is working a railtour on 5th May 1959, run jointly by the Manchester and Stephenson Locomotive Societies. (B.Hilton/M.J.Stretton coll.)

56.   Moving a few yards east, we encounter the water tank and column. The end of the branch is in the foreground, marked by an inverted chair. The end operationally was on 2nd December 1963, although passenger traffic ceased in 1932. (H.C.Casserley)

57.   We now move along the route towards the quarries; the rain was falling on 17th July 1963. The entire route had been inherited by BR. We are at the fold in the map, but the B4418 on the right had not been built when it was published. We are at the gateway to the goods yard and are looking east, up the valley. (R.M.Casserley)

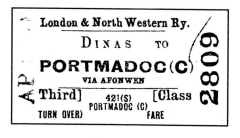

London & North Western Ry.

DINAS   TO

PORTMADOC (C)

VIA AFONWEN

Third]   421(S)   [Class
PORTMADOC (C)
TURN OVER)   FARE

AP   2809

L.   M.   &   S.   R.
Issued subject to the conditions & regulations in
the Co. Time Tables Books Bills & Notices & in the
Railway Co's Book of regulations relating to traffic
by Passenger Train or other similar service.

PANT GLAS   TO

YNYS

THIRD]
CLASS]   718(S)   FARE 16/10
YNYS

58.   The first incline is seen on 23rd September 1958. The track was complete to Pen yr Orsedd until 1963. This quarry was worked until 1984, but internal steam traction ended in 1960. (R.M.Casserley)

59.   Two horses sufficed for most slate traffic until 1959 and the subsequent mechanical power was provided for a railtour on 2nd October 1963. The SLS and MLS organised it again. Many quarries had tracks of both narrow gauges. (A.M.Davies)

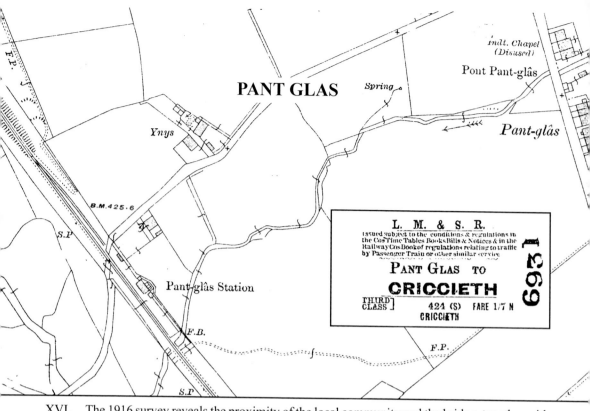

PANT GLAS

Ynys

B.M.425.6

S.P

Pant-glâs Station

F.B.

S.P

Spring

Pont Pant-glâs

Indt. Chapel
(Disused)

Pant-glâs

F.P.

L. M. & S. R.
Issued subject to the conditions & regulations in
the Cos Time Tables Books Bills & Notices & in the
Railway Cos Book of regulations relating to traffic
by Passenger Train or other similar service

PANT GLAS TO
CRICCIETH
THIRD] 424 (S) FARE 1/7 N
CLASS] CRICCIETH

6931

XVI. The 1916 survey reveals the proximity of the local community and the bridge, together with the spelling at that time. The siding lasted until 2nd June 1952. The house north of the station was for the station master. The opening date is not certain, but a regular service was shown from June 1872.

60. A rare staff photograph from 1914 includes a station master with a uniform problem and a frame with two levers out of use - the white ones. The building was of similar style to those on the NWNGR. (K.Robinson coll.)

61.　　Closure came on 7th January 1957, the village having a good bus service at its centre. The gate post seems to have been assaulted. The summit of the route was two miles north of the station. (J.Moss/R.S.Carpenter coll.)

62.　　This hut was built over the exposed 4-lever frame in 1956 and was retained for the crossing keeper until the end, but the old building was demolished. The signals protected the gates and were upper quadrant from 1952. We are now over 400ft above sea level. (Lens of Sutton coll.)

BRYNKIR

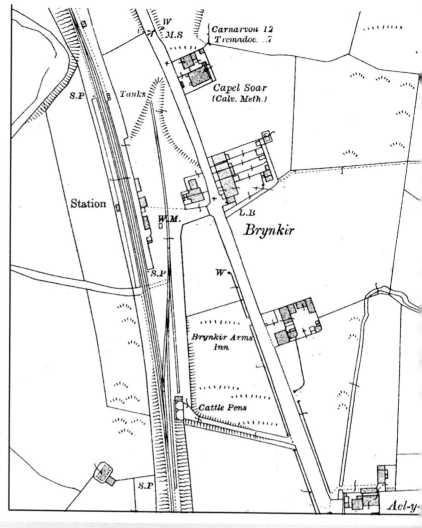

XVII. The 1918 survey includes cattle pens; there was a cattle market nearby.

63. A severe storm caused this damage to a bridge just south of the station, in June 1935. It was near Llecheiddior and was over the Afon Dwyfach, which was only about three miles from its source at this point. A member of staff walked over this shortly before the collapse, to stop the 5.14am from Caernarvon.
(K.Robinson coll.)

64.   The loop was provided at the opening of the line and, like the others, was extended twice. This northward view from around 1960 includes yellow brick quoins again. (J.Moss/R.S.Carpenter coll.)

65.   Two more views from the same era and this includes part of the goods yard. Service was withdrawn on 4th May 1964. The oil lamps were placed in the lanterns at dusk. (J.Moss/R.S.Carpenter coll.)

66.   Such installations were created before the age of vandalism and were accessed up three or four steps. This was the largest exposed frame and it had 16 levers when built. There was a camping coach nearby for many summers. (J.Moss/R.S.Carpenter coll.)

67.   A rare example of a tender engine was recorded in bad weather in July 1963. It is working a Penychain to Liverpool Lime Street train containing holidaymakers from Butlins. Such trains often had ten coaches. The cattle dock is on the left. (J.W.T.House/C.L.Caddy coll.)

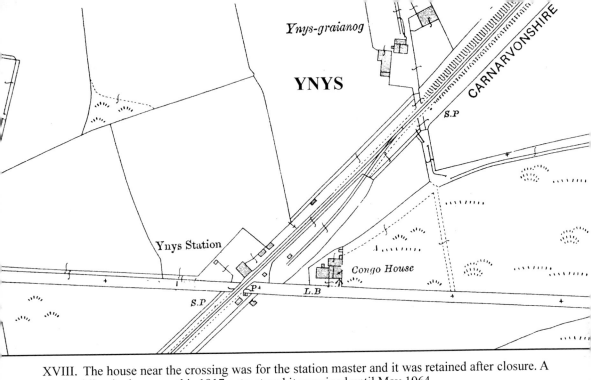

Ynys-graianog

YNYS

CARNARVONSHIRE

S.P

Ynys Station

Congo House

S.P   P   L.B

XVIII. The house near the crossing was for the station master and it was retained after closure. A single siding is shown on this 1917 extract and it remained until May 1964.

68.   The very low platform meant that portable steps had to be available upon demand. The siding is hidden by the shrubs on the right of this 1961 photograph. (Stations UK)

69.   All the buildings were of timber construction, except the house. Until January 1872, trains only stopped here on market days and they seem to have commenced in March 1869. (Lens of Sutton coll.)

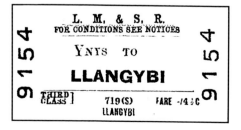

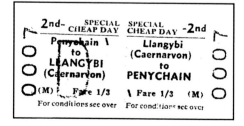

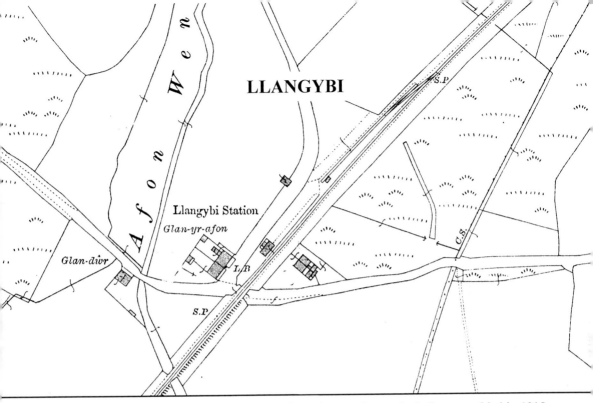

LLANGYBI

Llangybi Station

Glan-yr-afon

Glan-dŵr

XIX.   The 1917 edition does not include the down loop and second platform provided in 1915, as the survey was done before that time. The goods siding closed on 4th January 1954. Trains had first appeared in Bradshaw in October 1870 and called on Tuesdays only until January 1872.

70.   A conventional signal box was provided here and it contained 15 levers. It is seen from the south on 27th June 1956. Regular running of DMUs began in the November following, but only on a small proportion of services. (H.C.Casserley)

71.   Running over the level crossing on 8th August 1964 is a train from Butlins at Penychain. It was uncommon to have a tank and tender engine combination. Two tanks, bunker to bunker were often seen with long trains on Summer Saturdays. (D.A.Johnson)

72.   A Derby Lightweight DMU waits at the down platform, which was always devoid of any shelter. The local population was recorded as 522 in 1901. (K.Robinson coll.)

CHWILOG

XX. The suffix "for Nevin" was used in 1900-09 and thus does not show on this 1917 edition. The name of the river was the origin of the name of the next station. The main street was unusually straight for the mountainous area. It was intended as the main road to Ireland.

L. & N.W.R.
CARNARVONSHIRE BRANCH

Well

ial Ground

Weir

S.P

Afon Wen

C.R.

Mill Race

Sl

Ty'r-felin

Spring

Corn M

Capel Siloh
(Indt.)

Pont y
Felin

Sl

B.M 112.1 110 M.S

School

P

P.O.

Station

S.P   W.M

Bryn-awel

Porth Dinllaen 11
Portmadoc.......9½

Hotel

Smy

+100

Chwilog

S.P

Well

Traian

Cattle Pens

Spring

73. The second siding of the goods yard is on the far left, near the weighbridge office. The freight facilities were withdrawn on 4th May 1964. The lamp room is nearest and the porters room is next to it. (Lens of Sutton coll.)

74. The end of the cattle siding is in the right foreground and the goods yard is beyond, in this view from 27th June 1956. The house was for the station master and the structure this side of it was for gentlemen. The buildings were demolished in 1968. (H.C.Casserley)

↓ 75. The frame was recorded on 4th July 1965. What appears to be white levers were painted yellow and were used for the distant signals. (D.K.Jones coll.)

AFON WEN

76. An eastward panorama on 18th July 1941 shows LMS 2-6-2T no. 42 standing at the middle platform, having just arrived with the 12.45 from Bangor. It had been a down train, but, upon arrival here on GWR metals, it was termed an up one. (H.C.Casserley)

XXI. On the left of this 1917 map are two single lines: the upper one is for Bangor trains and the lower for Pwllheli ones. The turntable was little used and vanished in the 1930s. All the dwellings were for railway staff, the upper one being for the station master.

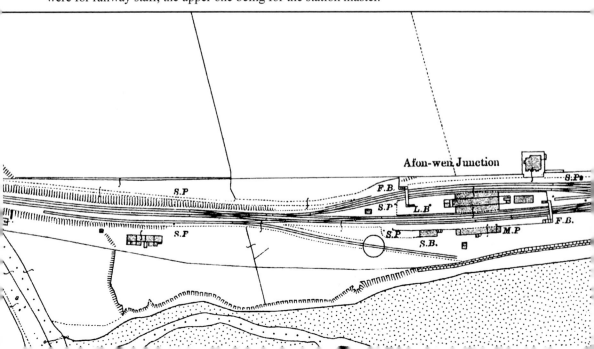

Afon-wen Junction

77.   A view in the other direction from the same footbridge has a BR 2-6-0 running into platform 3 with a train from Pwllheli. Few passengers joined trains here, but those who did had to use the path on the right and then the footbridge. (E.M.Johnson/Ted Hancock Railway Photographs)

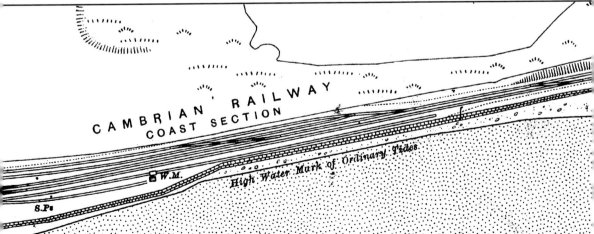

CAMBRIAN RAILWAY
COAST SECTION

High Water Mark of Ordinary Tides.

W.M.

S.Ps

s a n d

78.   A DMU waits to depart for Llandudno Junction, sometime in 1961. Assorted fire buckets hang on the end wall in the traditional fashion. (A.M.Davies)

79.   Most Bangor trains used the northern platform, No. 3. Waiting to depart from it is 2-6-4T no. 80104, which was built by BR at Brighton. Some trains reversed here to reach Butlins Holiday Camp at Penychain, which was less than one mile distant. A few continued to Portmadoc. (A.M.Davies)

↓ 80.   No. 1 platform is on the left in this westward view and the signal box is on it. The 75-lever frame was in use until 30th April 1967, but the station closed with the Bangor line on 7th December 1964. Only a fragment of platform remains, plus a single line.
(R.K.Blencoe/Ted Hancock Railway Photographs)

CRICCIETH

81.   Long after the building of its impressive castle, the town developed as a select holiday resort and residential area. A westward view in 1939, includes a weighing machine for the health minded. In the left distance was a bay, used for the occasional van. (Stations UK)

XXII.   The 1900 map at 20 ins to 1 mile has part of the elegant public gardens on the right, together with the footbridge used by those seeking the seafront. The headshunt ends nearby.

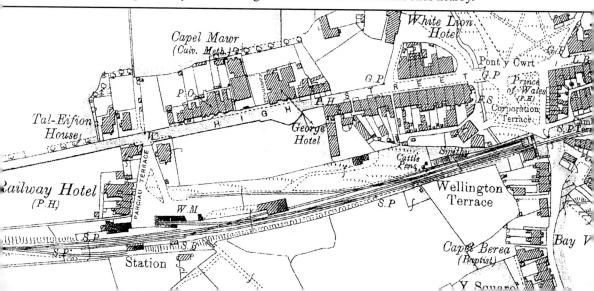

82.   Looking east in 1954, we can see the crossing provided for both barrows and passengers. The small goods yard is just out of view; this closed on 5th October 1964. There was a signal box on the far right until October 1977, when the loop was taken out of use. (H.C.Casserley)

83.   The spacious building was completed in 1873, six years after the line opened. It is seen in good condition in July 1988 and trains still call here. There was a London service in 1986, albeit Summer Saturdays only. (Ted Hancock Railway Photographs)

BLACK ROCK HALT

84.   Criccieth Castle is in the distance in this view from July 1965. The halt was opened adjacent to this foot crossing on 9th July 1923. It was a request stop used by visitors to Black Rock Sands and it closed on 13th August 1976, as the structure had rotted. (C.L.Caddy)

85.   Eastbound trains from the halt had a stiff climb at 1 in 54 inland and ex-GWR 2-6-2T no. 4560 is on the climb in July 1959. It will soon approach the site of Wern Siding, which served Wern Manor until 1957. (Ted Hancock Railway Photographs)

PORTMADOC

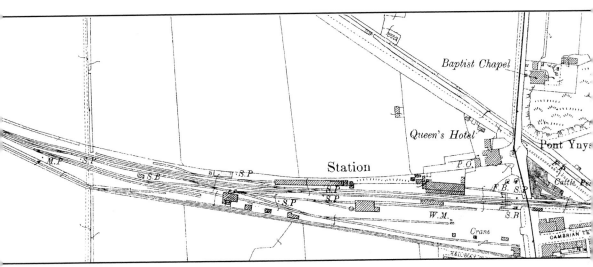

XXIII. The 1901 edition has the cattle pens, with two sidings, on the right. The long siding at the bottom is part of the Moel-y-Gest Tramway, which carried granite. A spur from it passes through a gate into the GWR yard. The scale is 20ins to 1 mile.

86.   The water tank is on the right and the engine shed is in the distance in this westward panorama from July 1948. The gable end of the goods shed is on the left.
(R.G.Nelson/T.Walsh coll.)

87. The map shows the footbridge to be at the far end of the platforms. This one was also little used and removed. The date is about 1953. (M.J.Stretton coll.)

88. The granite of Moel-y-Gest is in the background, as ex-GWR 0-6-0 no. 3202 waits to pass over the level crossing with freight on 24th August 1954. All trains from Bangor terminated here, as that was part of the agreement with the GWR and habits last. (H.C.Casserley)

89.   Foremost on 2nd July 1955 is BR 2-6-0 no. 78000. The shed closed in August 1963. Most of the 14 crews worked on the Cambrian Coast, but some were rostered to Bangor. (G.Adams/M.J.Stretton coll.)

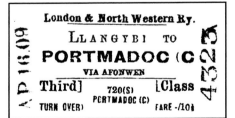

London & North Western Ry.

LLANGYBI   TO

PORTMADOC (C

VIA AFONWEN

Third]   720(S)   [Class

TURN OVER)   PORTMADOC (C)   FARE -/10½

AP 16.09   4323

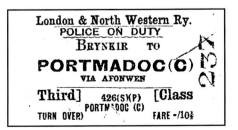

London & North Western Ry.
POLICE ON DUTY

BRYNKIR   TO

PORTMADOC(C)

VIA AFONWEN

Third]   426(S)(P)   [Class

PORTMADOC (C)
TURN OVER)   FARE -/10½

237X

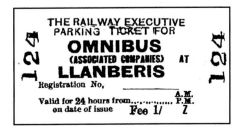

THE RAILWAY EXECUTIVE
PARKING TICKET FOR

OMNIBUS
(ASSOCIATED COMPANIES)   AT
LLANBERIS

Registration No,

Valid for 24 hours from.............. A.M.
on date of issue   Fee 1/   P.M.   Z

124   124

Other views of this station can be seen in pictures 68 to 76 in our *Barmouth to Pwllheli* album. The line from Afon Wen is included.

90.   A 1969 view west from the footbridge features the goods yard, which lasted until Barmouth Bridge was declared unsafe on 12th April 1980. The six remaining vans were removed by a diesel parcels unit, three at a time. They were for gunpowder traffic. Coal and feedstuff had been conveyed in small quantities, until that time. One siding was retained by the engineers and was used by steam trains running from Machynlleth each August from 2007. (K.Robinson)

91.   The 1894 box had 38 levers and was termed "East" until 1932. It is seen in May 1970. "West" is marked S.B. on the left of the map. The gates were replaced by barriers and the box closed on 23rd October 1988. The name had become Porthmadog on 5th May 1975, but the suffix "North" still remains to be added. (R.Ruffell/M.J.Stretton coll.)

2. Llanberis Branch

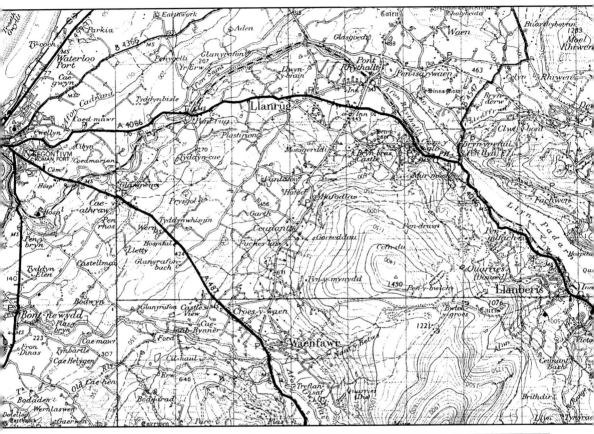

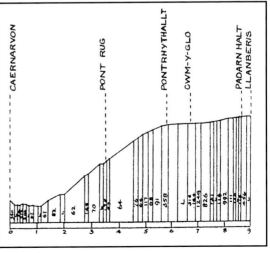

XXIV. Caernarvon is on the left and Llanberis on the right of this 1953 map at 1ins to 1 mile. The Padarn Railway is indicated as a mineral railway on the northeast side of Llyn Padarn, known now more frequently as Llanberis Lake. Excursion trains were common after regular services ceased in 1932. The terminus is below "Inn" and Padarn Halt is above it.

PONT RUG

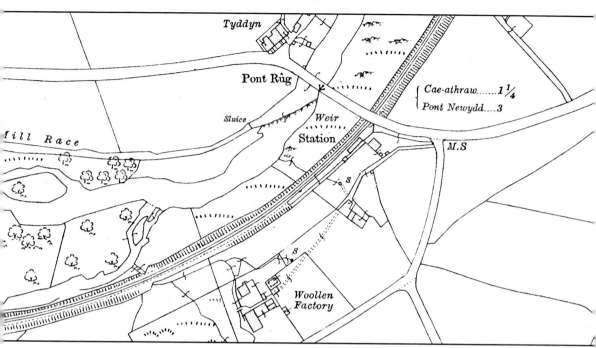

XXV. This little used station was closed as a wartime economy measure from 1st January 1917 until 1st July 1919. It is seen on the 1914 edition, close to the main road. This became the A4086 in 1919, after much wartime confusion.

92.   Closure was welcomed by locomotive crews no doubt, as the stop was mid-way on a three mile climb, much of it at 1 in 62 or 64. The building survived as a dwelling and was photographed in 1958. Regular trains ceased to call here after 22nd September 1930. (W.A.Camwell/S.L.S. coll.)

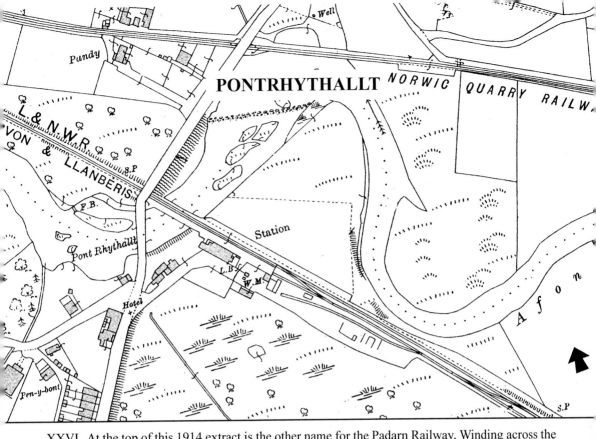

XXVI. At the top of this 1914 extract is the other name for the Padarn Railway. Winding across the map is the wide Afon Rhythallt, which drains Llyn Padarn.

93.　　The eight-lever open ground frame is obscured by the two men at the end of the bridge. Beyond the goods shed is a 5-ton crane. Nearest is the lamp room and coal store. Closure to regular passengers came on 22nd September 1930. (Lens of Sutton coll.)

94. The station opened a few months after the branch and was recorded in the 1960s, partially boarded up. The bridge over the river is on the right. The building is now a private house.
(Lens of Sutton coll.)

95. Turning round, we note that the goods shed and loading gauge had been removed. Only loaded wagons were handled and this traffic ceased on 7th September 1964.
(Lens of Sutton coll.)

CWM-Y-GLO

96. This was the busiest station on the branch before the coming of buses. The booking hall and office was under the nearest roof and the dwelling was under the far one. The roofless area was used by gentlemen and for secure coal storage. Very few excursion trains stopped at the low platform after World War II.
(Lens of Sutton coll.)

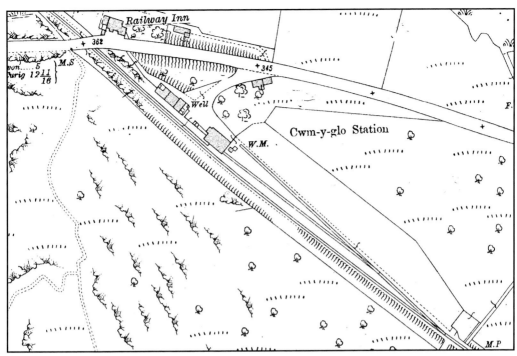

XXVII. The land surrounding the station during the 1914 survey was mostly marshy or rocky. There is a small shop at the junction of the road and the station approach.

97.   All items were lost in the 1980s, in favour of a bypass. An excursion is returning from Llanberis behind 2-6-4T no. 42198 on 16th August 1962. Many such trains originated at Rhyl by that time. Closure dates are as in captions 93 and 95. (Ted Hancock Railway Photographs)

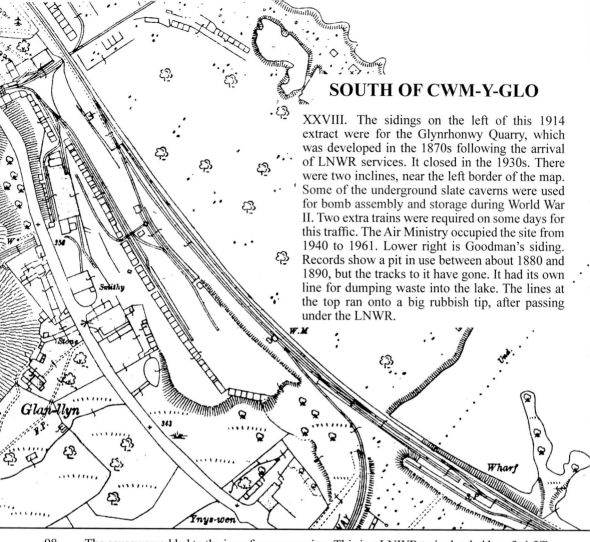

SOUTH OF CWM-Y-GLO

XXVIII. The sidings on the left of this 1914 extract were for the Glynrhonwy Quarry, which was developed in the 1870s following the arrival of LNWR services. It closed in the 1930s. There were two inclines, near the left border of the map. Some of the underground slate caverns were used for bomb assembly and storage during World War II. Two extra trains were required on some days for this traffic. The Air Ministry occupied the site from 1940 to 1961. Lower right is Goodman's siding. Records show a pit in use between about 1880 and 1890, but the tracks to it have gone. It had its own line for dumping waste into the lake. The lines at the top ran onto a big rubbish tip, after passing under the LNWR.

98.   The causeway added to the joy of any excursion. This is a LNWR train, hauled by a 2-4-2T. The Padarn Railway was on the far side of the lake. (R.M.Casserley coll.)

PADARN HALT

99.   The halt was opened on 21st November 1936 for the benefit of local residents, not tourists, and was closer to the town centre than the terminus. It appears on map XXIV.
(Lens of Sutton coll.)

100.   Part of the platform was still standing in June 1956. It had been used by a market day (Saturday) service to Caernarvon until September 1939, but it did not appear in Bradshaw.
(H.C.Casserley)

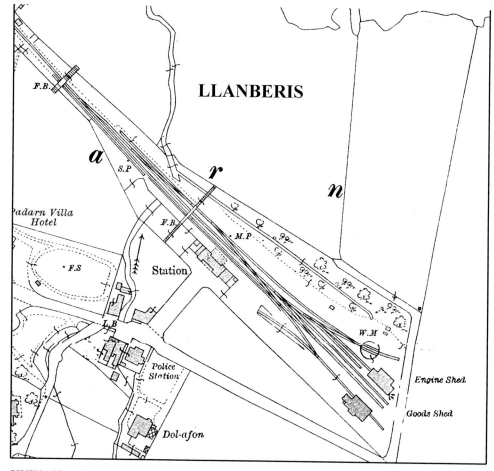

LLANBERIS

a S.P *r* *n*

Padarn Villa
Hotel

F.B.

F.B.

M.P

• F.S

Station

L.B

W.M

Police
Station

Engine Shed.

Goods Shed

Dol-afon

XXIX. The 1914 edition shows a wide approach road from the main road and two footbridges linking open spaces. The turntable was a 42ft model.

101.   This low quality postcard is included as it shows the engine shed in the centre distance and the goods shed to the right of it. The former closed in about 1915 and was demolished by 1919. (Lens of Sutton coll.)

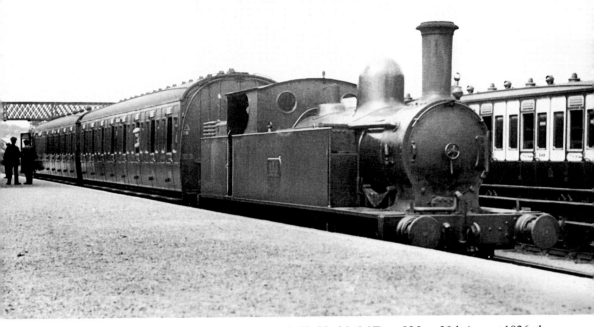

102.	The 1.0pm from Caernarvon was recorded behind 0-6-0T no. 835 on 30th August 1926; the door is open on the driving compartment used for the return journey. A note records that the third class coach on the right had been built in May 1888. (H.C.Casserley)

103.	The rest of our survey was undertaken in about 1951. The station was well conserved considering that there had been no regular passengers for around 20 years. In the left background is the water tank and a camping coach stands near the goods shed. (J.Moss/R.S.Carpenter coll.)

104. The small ground frame was at the far end of the canopy, shown in the previous picture. This structure had been rebuilt in a longer and narrower form. A DMU ran from Llandudno on Sundays in August 1961, but was not popular. (J.Moss/R.S.Carpenter coll.)

105. In the distance is the goods yard, which closed on 7th September 1964. A second camping coach was positioned at the opposite end of the site. On the right is a platform at which excursion trains would stop for ticket collection and then pull into the main platform. (J.Moss/R.S.Carpenter coll.)

106.   We return to the other end of the station to examine a fine LNWR observation car, one of which survives on the Bluebell Railway. As the locomotive returned to Caernarvon for servicing during the day, it took the coach with it for turning on the turntable. The car ran here from 1948 until 1962. (J.Moss/R.S.Carpenter coll.)

107.   The station closed to regular passenger trains on 12th September 1932, but excursions continued. They were suspended during WWII and were operated again from 6th July 1949 until 7th September 1962. The Hillman exhibits wartime limited lighting and wooden body. The building survives as a cafe and craft centre, with the main road on the former trackbed. (J.Moss/R.S.Carpenter coll.)

3. Llanberis Lake Railway

Llanberis

108. We start our journey at the most recent station. It was opened on 6th June 2003 and was built close to the main road. It was necessary to construct a lattice girder bridge over the short river feeding Llyn Padarn from Llyn Peris. (P.O'Callaghan)

XXX. Most passengers commence their journey at Gilfach Ddu, where there is an extensive car park. The train first proceeds to the terminus at Llanberis where more passengers are collected. The locomotive runs round the train and it then proceeds non-stop to the other terminus at Penllyn. Another run round takes place, but as there is no platform here, we show no photograph. The first call is at Cei Llydan and then there is a prolonged stop at Gilfach Ddu for coal and water before reaching Llanberis again. Overall journey time is 1hr. 10 mins. (Ll LR)

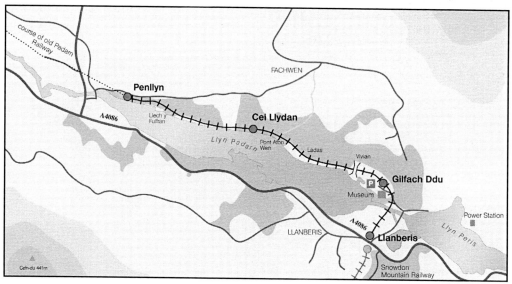

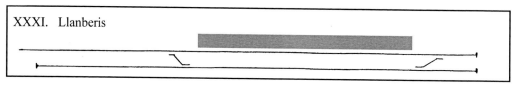

XXXI. Llanberis

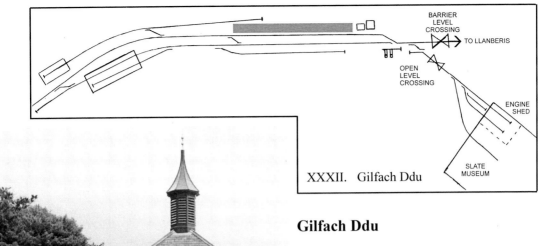

XXXII. Gilfach Ddu

Gilfach Ddu

109.   Dinorwic Quarry closed in July 1969,
steam having been used on the site until
October 1967. The main workshop area was
taken over by the National Museum of Wales
as a slate museum and part of it was used for Ll
LR locomotives. An 0-4-0ST Hunslet of 1889,
no. 1 *Elidir*, is about to enter it on 5th August
1992. The line has three 0-4-0STs and four
diesels. (P.G.Barnes)

110.   No. 2 *Thomas Bach* runs round its train
on 30th August 1998. This had been built by
Hunslet in 1904. The station was generally
called Llanberis until the new terminus opened.
(V.Mitchell)

111. *Elidir* is leaving Gilfach Ddu on 5th August 1992 with the carriage shed on the right and the permanent way facilities on the left. (P.G.Barnes)

112. No. 3 *Dolbadarn* was built in 1922 and is near Gilfach Ddu on 30th May 1979, with the main attraction on the left. Llanberis Lake is more correctly known as Llyn Padarn. (T.Heavyside)

Cei Llydan 113. No. 3 is seen again on the same day. This is a recommended picnic location and the starting point for superb walks in Padarn Park. The train is on its return journey. (T.Heavyside)

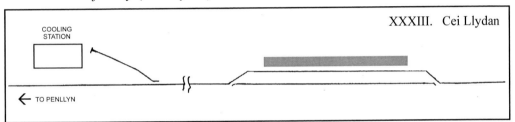

COOLING STATION

XXXIII. Cei Llydan

← TO PENLLYN

114. On the south side of the train are endless entrancing vistas across the beautiful lake. Looking north, one can glimpse this unmarked structure, which houses pumps of an unusual nature. The country's largest pumped storage power station (Dinorwic) is hidden under the mountains north of Llanberis and its six 400 kV output cables are underground, close to the railway. They have to receive cooling water and rail transport was provided to the circulating system, during its installation and maintenance. The photograph was taken in August 1998. (V.Mitchell)

4. Snowdon Mountain Railway

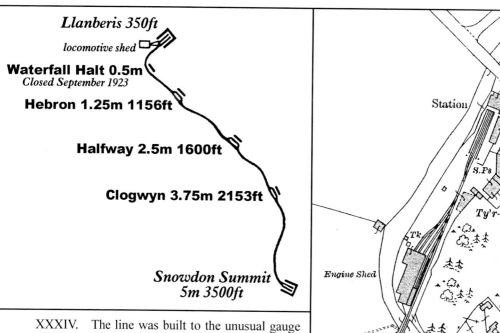

Llanberis 350ft
locomotive shed
Waterfall Halt 0.5m
Closed September 1923
Hebron 1.25m 1156ft
Halfway 2.5m 1600ft
Clogwyn 3.75m 2153ft
Snowdon Summit
5m 3500ft

Pont Victoria
Station
S.Ps
Ty'r-clwb
Engine Shed
S.P
Bryniau-ger

XXXIV. The line was built to the unusual gauge of 2ft 7½ ins for the reason that the locomotives were constructed in Switzerland to their standard of 800mm. The opening was in April 1896, but closure was immediate following a spectacular derailment, which destroyed locomotive no. 1 and its two coaches. Reopening was in April 1897.

XXXV. The 1914 map shows a layout which has remained virtually unchanged. The name of the company was the Snowdon Mountain Tramroad until 1928.

115. The terminus was photographed on 14th August 1953, with some of the upper levels of Dinorwic Quarry in the background. All trains were of one coach after 1897, with the locomotive at the lower end. (H.C.Casserley)

116.   The exterior was recorded on the same day. The railway ran for most of WWII, as there was military activity at the top of the mountain, except in 1944 when the line was closed. (H.C.Casserley)

117.   The outer end of the platform was photographed at the same time, along with the general manager's office, right. Above the other door are the words LADIES ROOM. Gentlemen were directed round the back. (H.C.Casserley)

118. The essential rack between the rails is more evident in this view of the shed area on 5th August 1992. It includes no. 4 *Snowdon* of 1896. Four of the five original engines survive, along with three from the 1920s, although some are in pieces. (P.G.Barnes)

119. No. 2 *Enid* exerts herself on the ascent on 10th August 1989, with Clogwyn station on the left. This is the only rack and pinion public railway in Britain and it provides a memorable experience with stunning panoramas. (T.Heavyside)

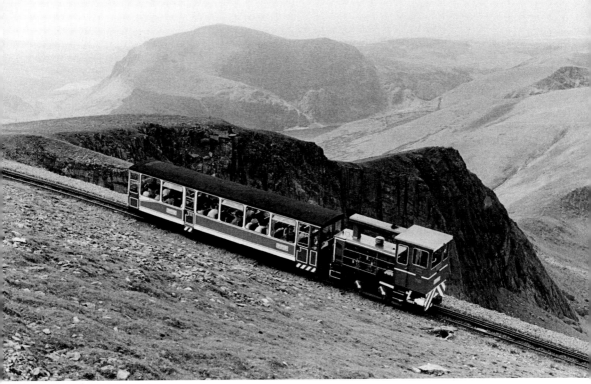

120.   No. 10 *Yeti* is nearing the summit on the same day. Hunslet provided four such diesel locomotives in 1986-92. One of the modern coaches is also to be admired, not to mention the vistas. The return journey takes about 2½ hours. (T.Heavyside)

121.   An entirely new summit station was constructed in 2008-09, but appears as a wall from the platforms. It opened on 12th June 2009. In attendance are no. 4 *Snowdon* and no. 2 *Enid*. Journalists reported that imported stone was used to build the new terminus. Local quarries provided 80% of the granite required, as the total demand was slightly in excess of their output within the seasonal time limits for construction. Long may the crowds support this unique venture. (SMR)

Middleton Press

EVOLVING THE ULTIMATE RAIL ENCYCLOPEDIA

Easebourne Lane, Midhurst, West Sussex.
GU29 9AZ   Tel:01730 813169

www.middletonpress.co.uk   email:info@middletonpress.co.uk
A-978 0 906520 B- 978 1 873793 C- 978 1 901706 D-978 1 904474
E - 978 1 906008 F - 978 1 908174

All titles listed below were in print at time of publication - please check current availability by looking at our website - *www.middletonpress.co.uk* or by requesting a Brochure which includes our *LATEST* RAILWAY TITLES also our TRAMWAY, TROLLEYBUS, MILITARY and COASTAL series